Adult Coloring Stress Relief

with Calming Card Games

Hearts

Copyright © Leaves of Gold Press 2015

All rights reserved. No part of this book may be reproduced or transmitted by any person or entity (including Google, Amazon or similar organisations) in any form or by any means, electronic or mechanical, including photocopying, recording or by any information storage and retrieval system, without prior permission in writing from the publisher.

Creator: Leaves of Gold Press - author.

Title: Adult coloring stress relief with calming card games: hearts /
Leaves of Gold Press ;
Elizabeth Alger, illustrator.
Series: Adult coloring stress relief ; 3
ISBN: 9781925110876 (paperback)
Target Audience: Adult.

Image on reverse of cards: 'Pimpernel' by William Morris

BISAC categories:
Self-Help / Self-Management / Stress Management
Self-Help : Creativity
Body, Mind & Spirit / Mindfulness & Meditation

Scan the QR code to visit Leaves of Gold Press

ABN 67 099 575 078
PO Box 9113, Brighton, 3186, Victoria, Australia
www.leavesofgoldpress.com

Ex Libris

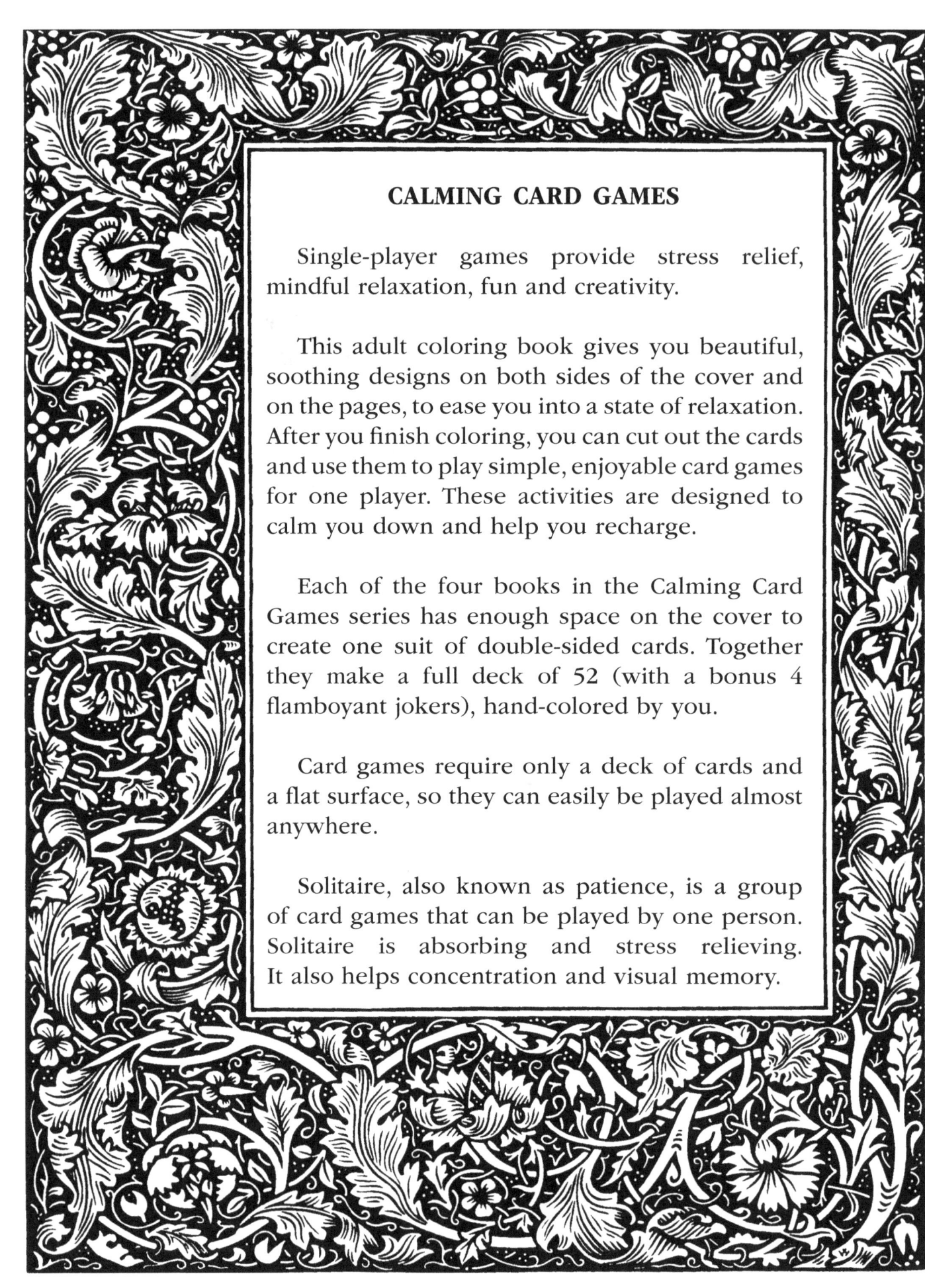

CALMING CARD GAMES

Single-player games provide stress relief, mindful relaxation, fun and creativity.

This adult coloring book gives you beautiful, soothing designs on both sides of the cover and on the pages, to ease you into a state of relaxation. After you finish coloring, you can cut out the cards and use them to play simple, enjoyable card games for one player. These activities are designed to calm you down and help you recharge.

Each of the four books in the Calming Card Games series has enough space on the cover to create one suit of double-sided cards. Together they make a full deck of 52 (with a bonus 4 flamboyant jokers), hand-colored by you.

Card games require only a deck of cards and a flat surface, so they can easily be played almost anywhere.

Solitaire, also known as patience, is a group of card games that can be played by one person. Solitaire is absorbing and stress relieving. It also helps concentration and visual memory.

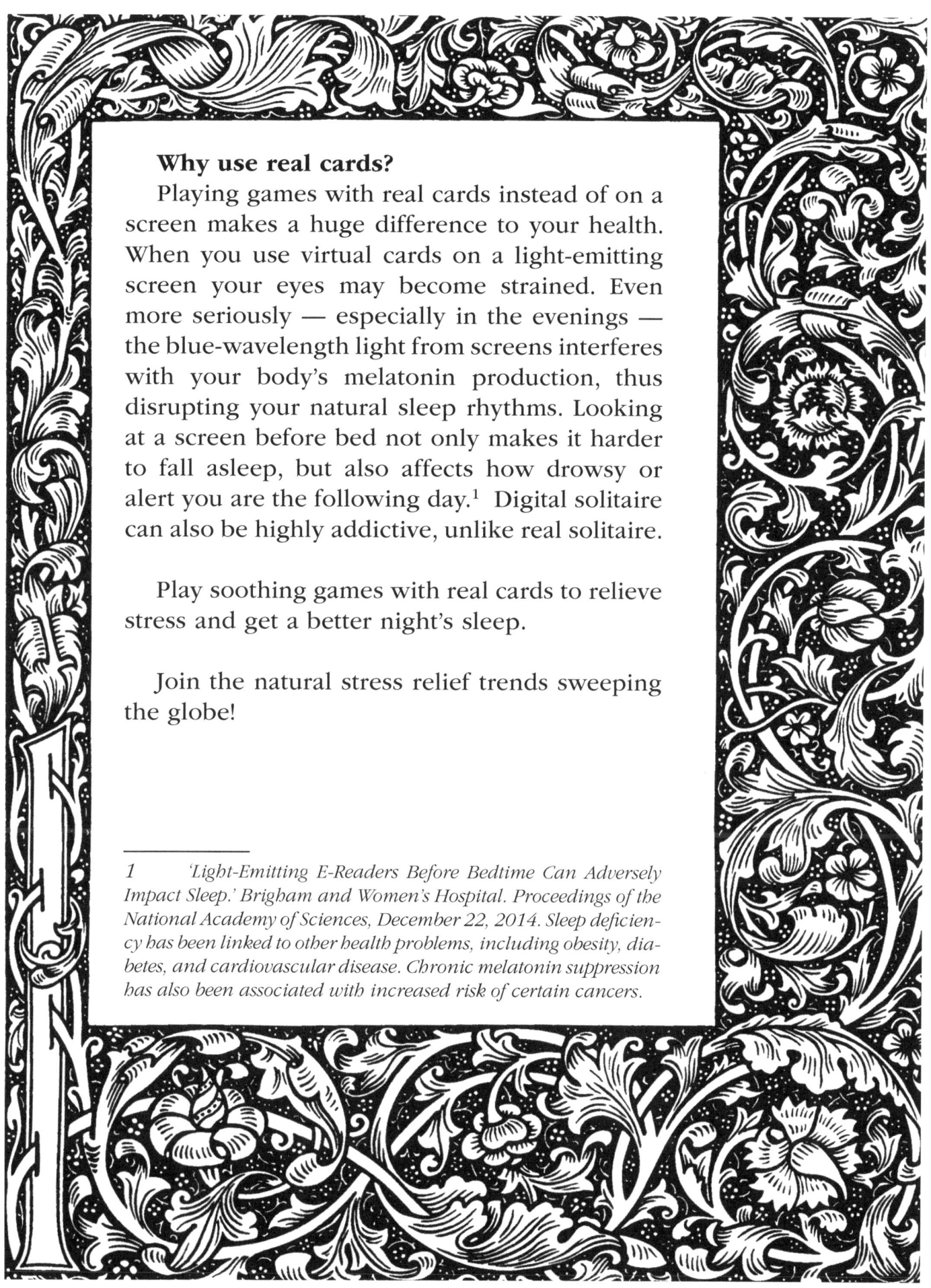

Why use real cards?

Playing games with real cards instead of on a screen makes a huge difference to your health. When you use virtual cards on a light-emitting screen your eyes may become strained. Even more seriously — especially in the evenings — the blue-wavelength light from screens interferes with your body's melatonin production, thus disrupting your natural sleep rhythms. Looking at a screen before bed not only makes it harder to fall asleep, but also affects how drowsy or alert you are the following day.[1] Digital solitaire can also be highly addictive, unlike real solitaire.

Play soothing games with real cards to relieve stress and get a better night's sleep.

Join the natural stress relief trends sweeping the globe!

---

1   'Light-Emitting E-Readers Before Bedtime Can Adversely Impact Sleep.' Brigham and Women's Hospital. *Proceedings of the National Academy of Sciences, December 22, 2014. Sleep deficiency has been linked to other health problems, including obesity, diabetes, and cardiovascular disease. Chronic melatonin suppression has also been associated with increased risk of certain cancers.*

THE SUIT OF HEARTS

The most popular European deck of playing cards is the set of 52 French cards. This comprises thirteen numerals of each of the four French suits; clubs, diamonds, hearts and spades. Each suit includes three 'court' or 'face' cards; king, queen and jack.

The Suit of Hearts is derived from the Suit of Cups, one of the four suits of Latin-suited playing cards. Cups are sometimes referred to as chalices or goblets.

In tarot, the element of cups is water, and the Suit of Cups relates to situations and events of an emotional nature, such as love. It is associated with the feudal class of 'clergy'.

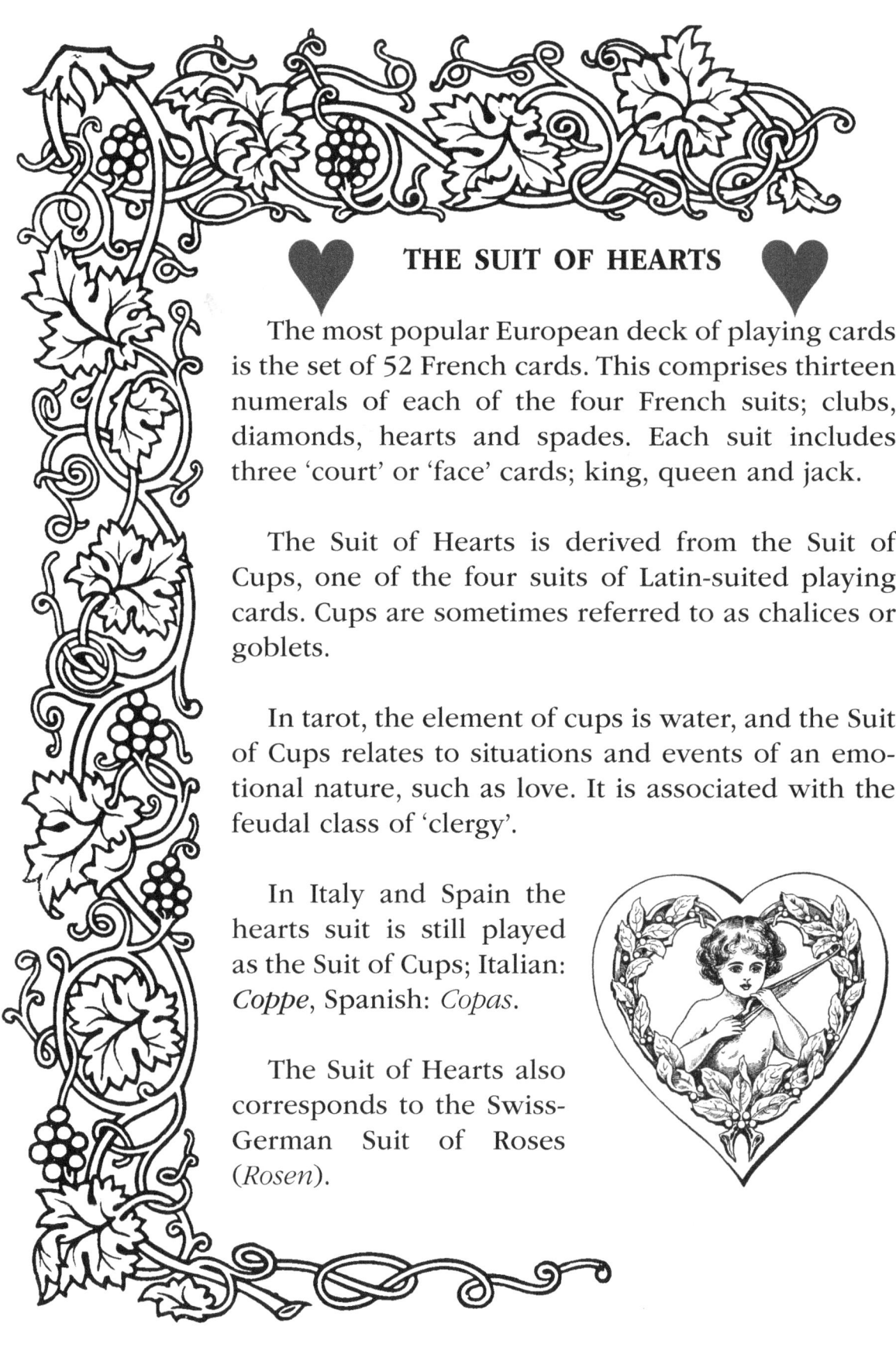

In Italy and Spain the hearts suit is still played as the Suit of Cups; Italian: *Coppe*, Spanish: *Copas*.

The Suit of Hearts also corresponds to the Swiss-German Suit of Roses (*Rosen*).

SOLITAIRE LAYOUT

Four types of card-piles exist in Solitaire:

- The Tableau: Seven columns of cards that constitute the main game on the table.

- The 'Foundation,' or 'Building' Piles: Four piles of cards, each of which contains cards of the same suit in a certain sequence. The suits are hearts, diamonds, spades and clubs. In most Solitaire/Patience games, the four aces are the bottom card in the pile, making the base of the foundations.

- The 'Stock', 'Draw' or 'Hand' Pile: This is the pile of cards that are left over after you have finished dealing out the cards for the tableau at the beginning of the game. Additional cards may be brought into play from this pile, according to the rules.

- The 'Talon', or "Waste" Pile: Any cards from the Stock pile that do not have a place in the tableau or on Foundation Piles are put face up in the Waste pile.

Layout for Klondike Solitaire

SOLITAIRE OR PATIENCE

Games of solitaire/patience generally involve re-arranging a layout of cards (called a 'tableau') with the aim of sorting them in some way.

There is a vast array of variations in one-player card games. The rules vary from simple to quite complex. Some use more than one deck of cards. This series of books, 'Adult Coloring Stress Relief with Calming Card Games' contains instructions for several of the most popular and relaxing games of solitaire, including:

- Klondike
- Accordion
- Flower Garden
- Spiderette
- Pyramid

Klondike is one of the most popular solitaire games. In Britain it may be called 'Canfield'. Klondike is also known as 'Fascination' and 'Demon Patience'.
Instructions follow.

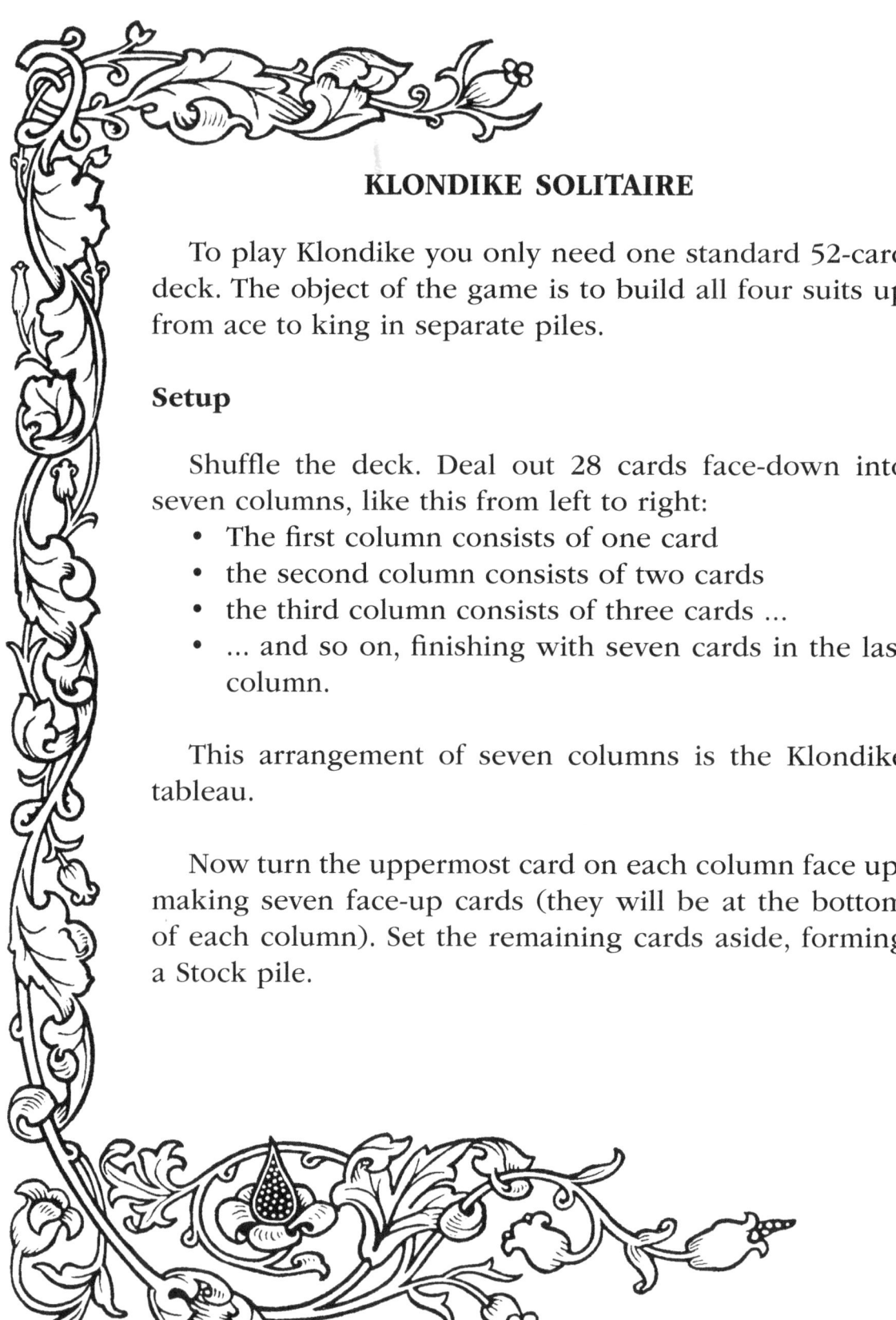

KLONDIKE SOLITAIRE

To play Klondike you only need one standard 52-card deck. The object of the game is to build all four suits up from ace to king in separate piles.

Setup

Shuffle the deck. Deal out 28 cards face-down into seven columns, like this from left to right:
- The first column consists of one card
- the second column consists of two cards
- the third column consists of three cards ...
- ... and so on, finishing with seven cards in the last column.

This arrangement of seven columns is the Klondike tableau.

Now turn the uppermost card on each column face up, making seven face-up cards (they will be at the bottom of each column). Set the remaining cards aside, forming a Stock pile.

Gameplay

Foundations:

Cards that are face-up can be moved from the Stock pile or the columns to the Foundation piles or to other columns.

Now, take a look at the cards that are face-up. Are there any aces showing? If so, move that ace out of the tableau and lay it down face-up to create the base of one of the four Foundation piles. All Foundation piles must begin with an ace!

Now that you have moved any aces that were showing, look for face-up cards with the value 2. Place these cards on top of the aces of the same suit in the Foundation piles.

To win Klondike you must move all the cards to the four Foundation piles. Each pile can only hold one suit and you must put the cards in the following order Ace, 2, 3, 4, 5, 6, 7, 8, 9, jack, queen and king.

Every time you move a face-up card out of a column, you need to turn the card beneath it face-up, so that the card can be played.

Always place each card in the columns so that every card below it remains partly visible. This way you can tell how many cards are in the column.

Once a card is moved to a Foundation pile, it cannot be removed.

Moving Cards within the Tableau:

The game also involves moving cards within the tableau itself. To move a card to a column, it must be one less in rank and the opposite color. For example, if you saw a face-up 10 of hearts (red), you could put a 9 of spades or clubs onto it.

Piles of cards may be moved from one column to another as long as they keep the same order — highest to lowest, and alternating colors.

If one column becomes empty, you can begin a new column with a king. Any new column must be started with a king, or a pile of cards that begins with a king.

The Stock and Waste Piles:

Once you have made all possible moves, start using the cards from the Stock pile, taking them from the top of the pile one by one. If there is nowhere for you to put that card, place it face-up onto the Waste pile. The top card of the Waste pile then becomes available to be played.

If you run out of Stock cards, turn the Waste pile over to make a new Stock pile and start again.

Winning

You win Klondike solitaire by building all four suits up from ace to king on the Foundation piles.

Variations of Klondike

- Play it the same way but with two decks, using 9 columns and 8 foundations.

- If you wish to make the game easier, instead of moving opposite *colors* to the columns, allow cards of different *suits* to be moved. This way, for example, an 8 of hearts could be placed onto a 9 of diamonds. Also, allow for any card to start a new column in an empty column space (rather than just the king).

- If you like, five rounds can make a game. Add up the number of foundation cards you have built up in each round to get your final score.

- Some versions of Klondike Solitaire allow you to move cards back and forth between the foundations and the tableau. This rule makes the game somewhat easier to win.

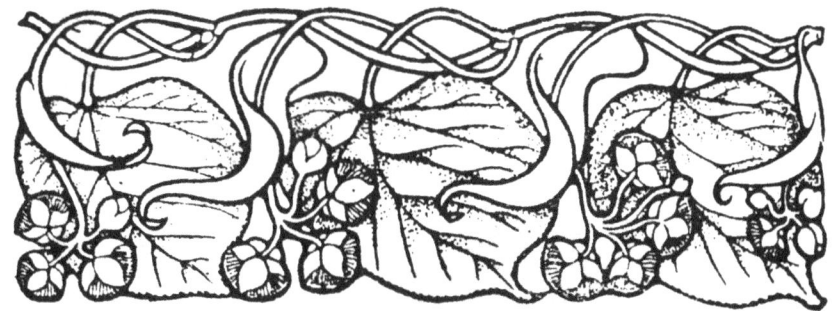

ADULT COLORING STRESS RELIEF: THE SERIES

Book 1: Adult Coloring Stress Relief with Calming Paper Crafts

Book 2: Adult Coloring Stress Relief with Calming Card Games: Spades

Book 3: Adult Coloring Stress Relief with Calming Card Games: Hearts

Book 4: Adult Coloring Stress Relief with Calming Card Games: Diamonds

Book 5: Adult Coloring Stress Relief with Calming Card Games: Clubs

IS FOOD MAKING YOU SICK?

People all over the world suffer from histamine intolerance without being aware of it.

We itch, sneeze, suffer from joint pain, inflammation, sleep disorders, irritability, anxiety, bowel disease, diarrhea, flatulence, stomach pain, heartburn and acid reflux, nausea, bloating and other digestive problems, eczema, psoriasis, tissue swelling, urticaria (hives), itching skin, itching scalp, sinusitis, runny nose, puffy eyes, hay fever, asthma, and breathing difficulties, or endure tension headaches, migraines, fuzzy thinking, dizziness, irregular heartbeat, painful periods (women), sudden drops in blood pressure, faintness or flushing.

Symptoms may endure throughout our entire lives if we continue to consume large amounts of histamine without knowing it. Histamine is colorless, odorless and tasteless — undetectable except by scientific analysis, and yet crucial to our well-being. Individual histamine tolerance thresholds vary greatly.

The good news is, if we can understand what is happening and why, we can treat or prevent this widely unrecognized condition. By far the best way to treat histamine intolerance (HIT) is with diet. All foods with the potential to raise histamine levels should be avoided until your health improves significantly.

This book discusses HIT in depth, including causes, symptoms and therapies, backed by scientific research. Along with a list of foods to help HIT sufferers, it includes a wide range of recipes for everything from entrées to desserts.

Find out more at www.low-histamine.com

THE SLEEP-INDUCING BEDTIME STORY

Children sometimes find it hard to get to sleep.

What if you could read them a bedtime story incorporating powerful psychological methods to help them fall asleep quickly, easily and without drugs?

Psychological sleep induction techniques include:
- putting aside your thoughts until the following day
- breathing deeply
- slowing down
- imagining a descent with the sensation of sinking
- progressive muscle relaxation
- using sleep-triggering words
- visualizing a safe and peaceful place
- employing the 'infectiousness' of yawning.

Such methods are well-known and can be found in libraries or by searching for 'psychological sleep techniques' on the Internet.

This book also uses the hypnotic power of rhyme and rhythm. Songs and lullabies have traditionally been used to lull children to sleep. 'Hypnotic' poetry works in much the same way.

The poems in this book are in the relaxing, calming rhythm called 3/4 time, better known as 'waltz time'. All parents know that gentle, rocking rhythms can soothe a child.

The rhyming is as important as the rhythm.

Children love poems that rhyme. For them, rhyming words make poetry fun and memorable. Just as children respond to Forssen Ehrlin's sleep-inducing story of Roger the Rabbit (the inspiration for this book), so they can fall asleep while listening to the tale of Misti the Kitty.

 # 1 New Release on Amazon in 'Sleep Disorders'.

www.ingramcontent.com/pod-product-compliance
Lightning Source LLC
LaVergne TN
LVHW070116080426
835507LV00043B/3492